29 TOP HITS FOR
TROMBONE

W9-CVU-518

PAGE	TITLE	ARTIST
2	ALL ABOUT SOUL	Billy Joel
4	ALL FOR LOVE	Bryan Adams, Rod Stewart & Sting
5	ALL THAT SHE WANTS	Ace Of Base
6	ANOTHER SAD LOVE SONG	Toni Braxton
7	BED OF ROSES	Bon Jovi
8	BREATHE AGAIN	Toni Braxton
9	CAN'T HELP FALLING IN LOVE	UB40
10	COME UNDONE	Duran Duran
11	DREAMLOVER	Mariah Carey
12	FIELDS OF GOLD	Sting
13	FOREVER IN LOVE	Kenny G
14	HAVE I TOLD YOU LATELY	Rod Stewart
15	HERO	Mariah Carey
16	HOPELESSLY	Rick Astley
17	I DON'T WANNA FIGHT	Tina Turner
18	I'D DO ANYTHING FOR LOVE (But I Won't Do That)	Meat Loaf
20	IF I EVER LOSE MY FAITH IN YOU	Sting
21	IN THE STILL OF THE NITE (I'll Remember)	Boyz II Men
22	LOOKING THROUGH PATIENT EYES	P.M. Dawn
23	ORDINARY WORLD	Duran Duran
24	RAIN	Madonna
25	REASON TO BELIEVE	Rod Stewart
26	THE RIVER OF DREAMS	Billy Joel
27	RUN TO YOU	Whitney Houston
28	SIMPLE LIFE	Elton John
29	TELL ME WHAT YOU DREAM	Restless Heart
30	TRUE LOVE	Elton John and Kiki Dee
31	WHEN I FALL IN LOVE	Celine Dion & Clive Griffin
32	A WHOLE NEW WORLD (Aladdin's Theme)	Peabo Bryson & Regina Belle

HAL•LEONARD
CORPORATION

7777 W. BLUEMOUND RD. P.O. BOX 13819 MILWAUKEE, WI 53213

ALL ABOUT SOUL

Trombone

Words and Music by
BILLY JOEL

ALL FOR LOVE

(From Walt Disney Pictures' "THE THREE MUSKETEERS")

Trombone

Words and Music by BRYAN ADAMS,
ROBERT JOHN "MUTT" LANGE and MICHAEL KAMEN

Moderately (not too fast)

ALL THAT SHE WANTS

Trombone

Words and Music by JOKER, BUDDHA, LINN and JENNY

ANOTHER SAD LOVE SONG

Words and Music by BABYFACE
and DARYL SIMMONS

Trombone

BED OF ROSES

Trombone

Words and Music by
JON BON JOVI

BREATHE AGAIN

Words and Music by
BABYFACE

Trombone

CAN'T HELP FALLING IN LOVE

Trombone

Words and Music by GEORGE DAVID WEISS,
HUGO PERETTI and LUIGI CREATORE

COME UNDONE

Trombone

Written by
DURAN DURAN

DREAMLOVER

Trombone

Words and Music by MARIAH CAREY
and DAVE HALL

FIELDS OF GOLD

Words and Music by
STING

Trombone

FOREVER IN LOVE

Trombone

By KENNY G

HAVE I TOLD YOU LATELY

Words and Music by
VAN MORRISON

Trombone

Slowly, with expression

HERO

Trombone

Words and Music by MARIAH CAREY
and WALTER AFANASIEFF

HOPELESSLY

Trombone

Words and Music by RICK ASTLEY
and ROB FISHER

Moderately slow rock

I DON'T WANNA FIGHT

(From The Touchstone Motion Picture "WHAT'S LOVE GOT TO DO WITH IT")

Trombone

Words and Music by BILLY LAWRIE,
LULU FRIEDA and STEVE DU BERRY

I'D DO ANYTHING FOR LOVE
(But I Won't Do That)

Trombone

Words and Music by
JIM STEINMAN

IF I EVER LOSE MY FAITH IN YOU

Trombone

Words and Music by
STING

IN THE STILL OF THE NITE
(I'll Remember)

Trombone

Words and Music by
FRED PARRIS

Moderately slow

Repeat and Fade

LOOKING THROUGH PATIENT EYES

(Contains sample from "FATHER FIGURE")

Trombone

Words and Music by ATTRELL CORDES
and GEORGE MICHAEL

MCA music publishing

ORDINARY WORLD

Trombone

Written by
DURAN DURAN

RAIN

Words and Music by SHEP PETTIBONE
and MADONNA

Trombone

Moderately, not too fast

REASON TO BELIEVE

Trombone

Words and Music by
TIM HARDIN

THE RIVER OF DREAMS

Words and Music by
BILLY JOEL

Trombone

RUN TO YOU
(From The Film "THE BODYGUARD")

Trombone

Words and Music by ALLAN RICH
and JUD FRIEDMAN

Moderately slow, tenderly

MCA music publishing

SIMPLE LIFE

Words and Music by ELTON JOHN
and BERNIE TAUPIN

Trombone

Moderately

TELL ME WHAT YOU DREAM

Trombone

Words and Music by JOSH LEO,
TIMOTHY B. SCHMIT and VINCE MELAMED

TRUE LOVE

Words and Music by
COLE PORTER

Trombone

WHEN I FALL IN LOVE

Trombone

Words by EDWARD HEYMAN
Music by VICTOR YOUNG

A WHOLE NEW WORLD (ALADDIN'S THEME)

(From Walt Disney's "ALADDIN")

Music by ALAN MENKEN
Lyrics by TIM RICE

Trombone